monsieur Marceau

LEDA SCHUBERT

ILLUSTRATED BY
GÉRARD DUBOIS

A NEAL PORTER BOOK
ROARING BROOK PRESS
NEW YORK

Look at this man.

He climbs imaginary stairs.

He bows to an invisible person.

He tames a lion no one can see.

He plays a violin that isn't there.

He does not speak.

His name is Marcel Marceau, and he is a mime.

He is the superstar of silence,

the maestro of mime—

acting without words.

He uses his whole body onstage:

his hands, his feet, his eyebrows, his toes,

his arms, his shoulders, his fingers, his nose,

but never his voice.

His body talks for him.

Who was this man who performed

on stages all over the world,

without speaking?

He was born Marcel Mangel in 1923 in Strasbourg, France,

a city close to the German border.

His family included dancers and musicians,

and his father, a butcher, had a fine voice.

Marceau loved the films of the time,

and he wanted to be like Charlie Chaplin,

the famous star of the silent movies.

When he was seven, he mimed in front of his friends to make them laugh.

But when he was sixteen, as World War II began, Marceau and his family were forced to move. The entire population of Strasbourg left by foot, train, or bus, carrying whatever they could.

Later, Marceau joined the French underground and its efforts to resist the Nazis.

He led hundreds of Jewish children

from an orphanage in France to safety in Switzerland.

They pretended they were going on vacation,

often disguised as boy scouts.

He helped hide American
parachutists in a French
monastery until the war ended.
Then he changed his last name
from Mangel to Marceau
so that people wouldn't know
he was Jewish.

His father died in the concentration camps. "The people who came back from the camps were never able to talk about it," Marceau later said. "My name is Mangel. I am Jewish. Perhaps that, unconsciously, contributed towards my choice of silence."

After the war, he studied mime.

When he was only

twenty-four, he created Bip.

The character would be part of

him for the rest of his life.

With his smashed stovepipe hat

and its red carnation,

his face caked in white makeup,

his eyebrows drawn high

on his forehead,

his red mouth,

and his sad eyes,

Bip searched for adventure

and got into trouble.

His fingers moved

as if made of rubber,

as if they had no bones.

Marceau became very famous.

Alone on stage,

a spotlight follows him.

He plays tug of war all by himself

with a rope that doesn't exist.

He fights a bull, picks a pocket,

hugs no one.

He chases butterflies without a net.

He walks against

the wind,

but there is no wind.

He can be a tree or a flower,

a fish or a human being.

He is full of joy

or full of sadness.

Sometimes he is one person
on stage—and sometimes many.
Sometimes there is music,
sometimes not.
He never loses the crowd's
attention.
He is a person like no other—
the world's most famous mime.
Think of the greatest movie star,
or music star, or sports star.
Marceau had no competition.
To list his prizes and awards
would take a very long time.

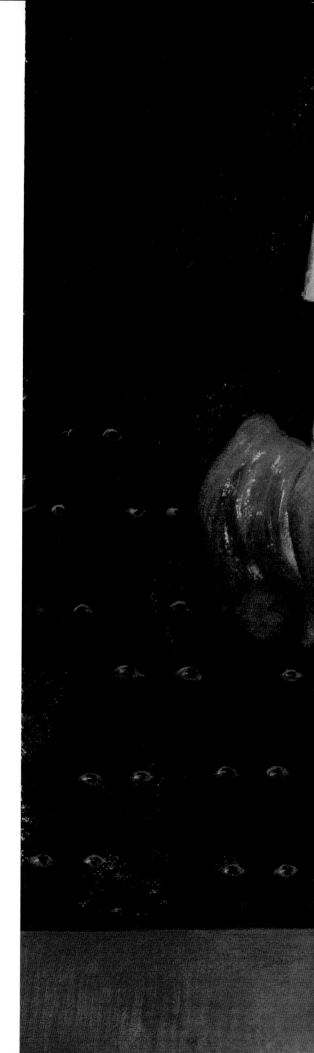

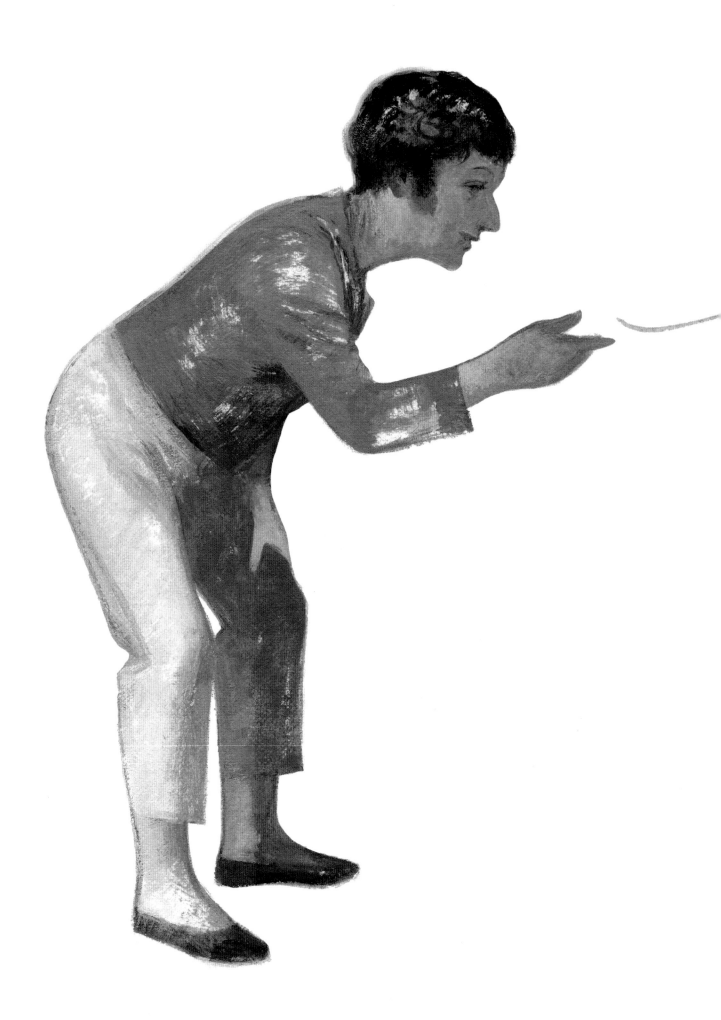

Offstage, he loved to talk.

He once said, "Never get a mime

talking. He won't stop."

He said, "The mime must make reality

into dreams and dreams into reality."

And he said, "Do not meddle in the

affairs of wizards, for you are crunchy

and taste good with ketchup."

In a silent movie,

when no one else spoke,

Marcel Marceau said one word,

"*Non.*" No.

He traveled the world—appearing
on television and on stage,
for presidents and princesses,
kings and queens, and
everyone else.
Marceau astonished audiences
from the United States to
Australia and from South
America to Japan. They all
understood his language.
He said, "Neither laughter
nor tears are French, English,
Russian, or Japanese."

The crowds who saw him
laughed and cried and knew
they had seen wonder.

AFTERWORD

Marcel Marceau, beloved by millions, was, and remains, the most famous mime in the world. During his lifetime, he gave over 15,000 performances, appearing as many as 300 times a year and touring throughout the world. He studied in Paris with the great Étienne Decroux, sometimes called "the father of modern mime," and later opened his own school.

Marceau was born in Strasbourg, France, in 1923. From early childhood, he was so good at making neighborhood children laugh that he planned to become the Charlie Chaplin of the theater. But the arrival of World War II changed his life. During that terrible war, Marceau joined the French underground. Using red crayon and ink, he altered the identity cards of children so they would appear to be too young to be sent to the labor camps. Then he took the incredible risk of leading Jewish children out of occupied France and over the high Alps to the safety of neutral Switzerland, saving the lives of hundreds.

During the war, he also began to use his body for powerful effects. "Marceau claimed he had learned the power of illusion on a sun-drenched afternoon toward the end of World War II while fighting with the French Resistance. He and a companion had entered a clearing and suddenly found themselves face-to-face with a unit of German soldiers. Startled, Marceau acted as if he was the advance guard of a larger French force and demanded the Germans surrender."

In 1947, Monsieur Marceau created his famous character, Bip, adapting the name from Pip in Charles Dickens's novel, *Great Expectations*. "Because when you are young, you have great expectations," Marceau said. But Pip in French sounds like peep, so he preferred Bip. Marceau performed the character in whiteface, and Bip became instantly recognizable, with his striped jersey and flower-bedecked top hat. The tradition of whiteface developed in the Italian *commedia dell'arte*, when a silly character who was a baker's assistant fell into the flour. The white face, which is put on with greasepaint, helps the audience view expressions from a distance. Marceau also performed entire dramas in mime without whiteface.

Mime, the art of nonverbal communication through gesture, began as far back as the ancient Greeks. There are mimes all over the world. Marceau said that to be a mime, one must be a painter, a writer, a sculptor, a poet, and a musician, and have both incredible stamina and talent.

Marceau died in 2007 and is buried in Père Lachaise cemetery in Paris.

Marcel Marceau visits Circus Smirkus in Vermont, 1999. Photo courtesy of Robert Sugarman.

Would you like to try mime yourself? Rob Mermin, the founding director of Circus Smirkus, a Vermont-based traveling circus (www.smirkus.org), studied extensively with Marcel Marceau and has some advice for getting started.

Pretend that there's a large refrigerator in front of you. Use your hands to outline the size.

Open the door.

Reach in for a banana and close the door.

Peel the banana.

Eat it.

Don't forget to throw away the peel!

Open the door again.

Reach in for a container of milk.

Close the door.

Pour the milk into an imaginary glass and drink it.

Don't forget to put down the container of milk before you drink!

Rob says that this exercise uses the senses of touch, sight, and taste. Use your imagination to feel the sweetness of the banana, the coldness of the milk, the weight of the glass, and the pleasure of the food in your tummy.

You might choose to identify with something in nature, becoming a tree as it grows from a seedling, drops its leaves in fall, feels the weight of winter snow, and opens up again in spring.

Or you might become a character: a pirate or a cowboy, a ballerina or a chef. How could you show others who you are?

Use your imagination to play with things that aren't there.

Can you play ball without a ball?

Can you fight with an umbrella in a rainstorm?

SOURCE NOTES

Page 19, "The people who came back from the camps . . ." Lichfield, John. "Silence falls on Marcel Marceau, master of the mime." www.independent.co.uk/arts-entertainment/theatre/news/silence-falls-on-marcel-marceau-master-of-the-mime-464626.html, September 4, 2007.

Page 35, "Never get a mime talking." U.S. News & World Report, February 23, 1987.

Page 35, "Do not meddle . . ." Crawford, Leslie. "Marcel Marceau." www.salon.com/people/bc/1999/07/27/marceau/, July 27, 1999.

Page 36, "Neither laughter nor tears . . ." Lust, Annette. *From the Greek Mimes to Marcel Marceau and Beyond.* Scarecrow Press: Lanham, 2003. p. ix.

Page 38, "Marceau claimed he had learned the power . . ." Ryback, Timother W. "Marcel Marceau and His Art." *International Herald Tribune*, September 24, 2007.

FURTHER READING

Lust, Annette. *From the Greek Mimes to Marcel Marceau and Beyond.* Scarecrow Press: Lanham, 2003.

Marceau, Marcel. *The Story of Bip.* Harper & Row: New York, 1976.

Marceau, Marcel and Bruce Goldstone. *Bip in a Book.* Stewart, Tabori & Chang: New York, 2001.

Martin, Ben. *Marcel Marceau, Master of Mime.* Optimum: Ottawa, 1978.

To my wordy sons, Thomas and Nathan —G.D.

To Steven Chudney for inspiration
To M. Porter, M. DuBois, and the Roaring Brook crew for the rest
Special thanks to Rob Mermin —L.S.

Text copyright © 2012 by Leda Schubert
Illustrations copyright © 2012 by Gérard DuBois
A Neal Porter Book
Published by Roaring Brook Press
Roaring Brook Press is a division of Holtzbrinck Publishing Holdings Limited Partnership
175 Fifth Avenue, New York, New York 10010
mackids.com

Library of Congress Cataloging-in-Publication Data
Schubert, Leda.
    Monsieur Marceau / Leda Schubert ; illustrated by Gérard DuBois.
        p. cm.
    Includes bibliographical references and index.
    ISBN 978-1-59643-529-2 (alk. paper)
    1. Marceau, Marcel—Juvenile literature. 2. Mimes—France—Juvenile
literature. I. Dubois, Gérard, 1968- ill. II. Title.
    PN1986.M3.S48 2012
    792.3092—dc23
    [B]
                                            2011033798

Roaring Brook Press books are available for special promotions and premiums.
For details contact: Director of Special Markets, Holtzbrinck Publishers.

First edition 2012
Book design by Jennifer Browne
Printed in China by South China Printing Co. Ltd., Dongguan City, Guangdong Province
10 9 8 7 6 5 4 3 2 1